Bill Will

by Liza Charlesworth • illustrated by Kelly Kennedy

SCHOLASTIC INC.

New York • Toronto • London • Auckland
Sydney • Mexico City • New Delhi • Hong Kong

Designed by Grafica, Inc.
ISBN: 978-0-545-68628-0
Copyright © 2009 by Lefty's Editorial Services.
All rights reserved. Published by Scholastic Inc.
SCHOLASTIC, LET'S LEARN READERS™, and associated logos are trademarks and/or registered trademarks of Scholastic Inc.

12 11 10 9 8 7 6 5 4 3 2 1   68   15 16 17 18 19 20/0

Printed in China.

The Ill Family

What Is a Word Family?
A word family is a group of words that rhyme and share the same spelling pattern, such as *Bill*, *will*, and *hill*. Read this story to learn more –*ill* words!

Meet **Bill**.
Bill is a member of the **Ill** family.

Bill never says, "I won't."
Bill always says, "I **will**."

Will Bill take his sister **Jill** up the **hill**?

Bill will.
What a **thrill**!

Will Bill fix Grandpa **Phill**'s broken **grill**?

Bill will.
He used a **drill**!

Will Bill try one of Grandma **Lill**'s super-sour **dill** pickles?

Bill will.

And he did not get **ill**!

Will Bill pour punch for little **Gill** and not even **spill**?

Bill will.
What **skill**!

Will Bill fill the **Ill**s' pool with water?

Bill will.
Time to **chill**!

Word Family House

Point to the *-ill* word in each room and read it aloud.

fill · dill · will

pill · mill · hill

grill · Bill · skill

still · spill

chill · thrill

Word Family Rhymes

Point to the rhyming pair that completes each sentence.

WORD BOX

gill chill   **dill thrill**

hill spill

grill skill   **ill pill**

1 A yummy pickle gives you a _____ _____.

2 A barbecue chef has _____ _____.

3 A cold fish can get _____ _____.

4 Jack and Jill had a _____ _____.

5 A sick person should take an _____ _____.

Word Family Hunt

This pool contains eight *-ill* words. Can you find them all? Cover them with pennies or buttons.

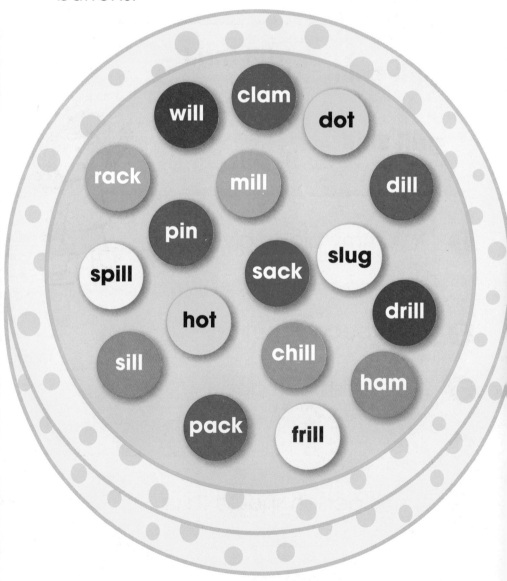